EXTRAORDINARY CONSERVATIVES

HOW THEY WON THE GENERAL ELECTION IN 2015

JOSHUA JOGO

Disclaimer

All the material contained in this book is provided for educational and informational purposes only. No responsibility can be taken for any results or outcomes resulting from the use of this material. While every attempt has been made to provide information that is both accurate and effective, the author does not assume any responsibility for the accuracy or use/misuse of this information.

Published in the United Kingdom by
Heathrow Gateway Publishing UK
HGPUK
Empowerment House
London.

Publishing rights administered on Amazon by HGPUK
All rights reserved

For Publisher Enquiries Contact:
HGPUK
Empowerment House
London
United Kingdom
Email: joshuajogo@hotmail.com

Presented To:

____

From:

____

Date:

____

Sign:

____

DEDICATION

To Terna Jogo my first daughter for successfully securing a place at the university in 2015 to study media and film.

Joshua Jogo Jnr and Terdoo Jogo, my twin children for successfully passing out of secondary school in 2015 in flying colours!

To my beloved wife, Lizzy Jogo who just celebrated her 47th Birthday on July 14th. May you be blessed among women!

ACKNOWLEDGEMENTS

I wish to acknowledge the following media sources who provided valuable resources and insight into the production of this book. The Daily Telegraph, The BBC News, CCN News London. Comres, UK Polling Report and Conservatives.com/sharethefacts.

CONTENTS

INTRODUCTION

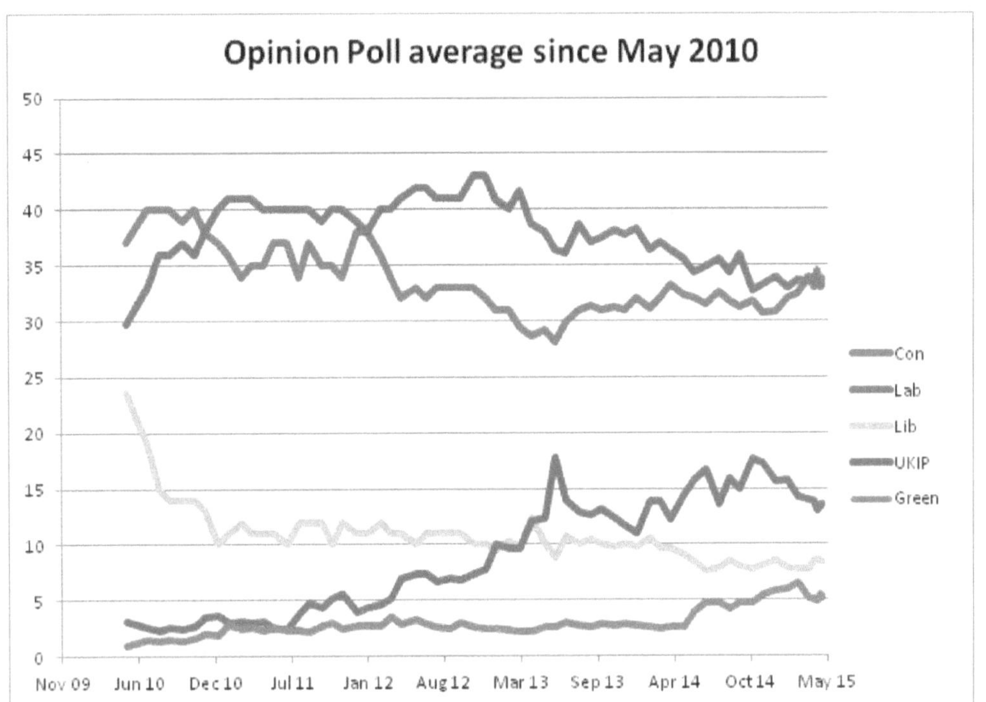

It all began with the apparent predictions of the pollsters. It's that time of the political moment when all the opinion polling companies and organisations get busier than the politicians. This year was going to be no different. Day in day out the polls kept coming in. According to opinion polls, it was a very tightly and closely fought election like no other. It was neck and neck they said. It was going to be another hung parliament and the list went on and on. It was meant to be the most unpredictable election in modern history, yet it was the most predictable election in opinion polling history.

WHAT HAPPENED? THE POLLS WERE WRONG!

How pollsters gravely underestimated conservative support in 2015 and risked the entire integrity of the opinion poll industry.

Those that follow polling closely will recall the famous situation in 1992 where the polls appeared to point to a Labour victory (of sorts) only for the Conservatives to prevail. Since that time, much work has gone into correcting those mistakes and subsequent election results have shown that the polling industry has been largely successful at achieving this.

However, in an election so close, with so many different parties (and pollsters) involved, could we face the prospect of history repeating itself? Here I examine some of the challenges pollsters face.

IT'S VERY CLOSE

Aside from the occasional poll showing a 6 point lead for Labour or the Conservatives, most national polls show the two main parties neck and neck. In fact, the current UK Polling Report average has Labour and the Conservatives on 34 points each. Therefore, by understating either the Labour or Conservative vote slightly, the polls could point to a completely different result to the one we see on Election Day. Indeed, some pollsters could easily call the election wrong (or right) by sheer accident of 'margin of error'. What is clear is that the apparent closeness of the race exacerbates the potential for the polls to be 'wrong'.

DEALING WITH A 'MULTI-PARTY' SYSTEM

In 1992, pollsters were mainly concerned with Labour, the Conservatives and the Liberal Democrats. Now, each of the SNP, UKIP and the Greens are important too. These parties are not just important for their own sake. Polls that overstate UKIP's support could also understate Conservative support and if Scottish polls overstate support for the SNP then Labour's situation north of the border could be better than current polling suggests (though still very bad). Therefore, not only is this election close but pollsters are also having to contend with several new variables this time around which are all important.

RETURN OF THE 'SHY TORIES'?

One of the major issues in 1992 was the so-called 'Shy Tory' phenomenon where voters told pollsters that they intended to vote Labour (or someone else) where in fact they actually intended to vote Conservative. If such a phenomenon repeats itself this could be crucial in such a close race. Former Conservative MP Rob Hayward has produced analysis (more here) showing that polls have regularly understated Conservative support this parliament when compared to the actual result in elections.

Could this happen again? It's possible. A key group to watch out for is the cohort of Labour supporters that consistently say that they would prefer David Cameron as Prime Minister. For example, the latest Ipsos Mori political monitor shows that some 28% of current Labour supporters say that they are dissatisfied with Ed Miliband's performance as Labour leader.

Miliband's ratings are of course improving during the campaign and it is debatable how much impact leader ratings have anyway. However, if we are looking for evidence of 'Shy Tories' then current Labour supporters unconvinced by Miliband would be an obvious place to start. We should remember, not all party 'supporters' in opinion polls are committed activists – some are floating voters liable to change their minds.

HOW MUCH SUPPORT DOES UKIP REALLY HAVE?

Arguably the biggest challenge faced by pollsters is calling UKIP's vote share correctly. Barring some significant polling convergence between now and voting day someone is going to be very wrong here. UKIP's support in opinion polls ranges from anywhere between 17% (Survation) and 7% (ICM) at present. Clearly, these both cannot be right. Also, like the SNP, UKIP relies on a significant number of previous non-voters for its support. Again, as with the SNP vote, it will be interesting to see if this support turns up on the day.

Returning to the differences in UKIP support between pollsters, it is interesting to compare levels of support achieved online compared to telephone polls. Below is a recent chart produced by Anthony Wells from YouGov that illustrates this point, consistent this parliament that UKIP tend to achieve greater levels of support online? Perhaps online polls are correcting a 'spiral of silence' among UKIP voters or perhaps they are overstating UKIP support. We will know soon enough. The point is that they are different and both cannot be right.

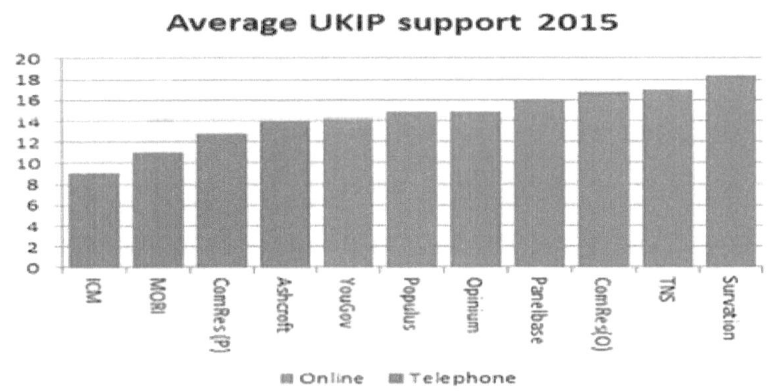

CHAPTER ONE

WHY THE OPINION POLLS GOT IT SO WRONG

YouGov president explains: Peter Kellner, president of YouGov, admits the polling firms who put Labour and the Tories neck and neck for months got it wrong.

The strength of the Conservative Party result has confounded predictions Photo: AFP

Months of extensive opinion polling were wrong about the election result, a senior pollster admitted as the strength of the **Conservative Party** result confounded predictions.

Opinion polls have consistently shown Labour and the Tories almost neck and neck for months, with little shift throughout the campaign.

Yet those polls by the early hours of Friday appeared to have significantly underestimated Conservative support and overestimated Labour support.

The size of the discrepancy saw comparisons with flawed polls from 1992, where surveys predicted a hung parliament, but the Conservatives won an outright majority.

Peter Kellner, president of YouGov, admitted the polling firms had got it wrong again.

Peter Kellner blamed politicians for relying too heavily on polling data during their campaigns (John Taylor/The Telegraph)

He said: "What seems to have gone wrong is that people have said one thing and they did something else in the ballot box."

He said: "We are not as far out as we were in 1992, not that that is a great commendation." But he blamed politicians for relying too heavily on polling data during their campaigns and said they should instead concentrate on standing on a platform of what they believe in. He said politicians "should campaign on what they believe, they should not listen to people like me and the figures we produce".

The **BBC** pundit was repeatedly asked to explain where the polls had gone wrong with the presenter David Dimbleby at one point saying that politicians would never take any notice of them again. The exit poll showing the Conservative Party on 316 seats and Labour on 239 seats was starkly at odds with polling during the election campaign, as well as two large-scale conventional surveys conducted after people had voted.

A YouGov ballot-day poll for the Sun of 6,000 people who had voted painted a much brighter picture for Mr Miliband, putting Labour and Tories tied on 34 per cent each, Ukip on 12 per cent, Lib Dems on 10 per cent, the SNP and **Plaid Cymru** on 5 per cent and Greens on 4 per cent.

A second survey of 12,000 voters for former Tory treasurer Lord Ashcroft put the share of votes at 34 per cent for Conservatives and 31 per cent for Labour, with

Ukip on 14 per cent, Lib Dems on 9 per cent and Greens and SNP each on 5 per cent.

3 ERRORS THE POLLSTERS MADE

When the exit poll dropped at 10pm the numbers seemed unbelievable. A few hours later and that forecast was looking overly cautious.

The initial figures, which predicted the Tories would win 316 seats, ended up underestimating the party. David Cameron won an overall majority – an outcome deemed near impossible based on pre-election polling.

It is clear that the polls and, as sure as night follows day, the forecasts modelled on polling, have had a bad election. The question is why did the polls get it wrong?

In the end, the debate over whether online or phone polls are better, and discussions about different methodologies to weight undecided voters and filter for certainty to vote, all proved irrelevant. Although phone polls during the course of the campaign had shown several Tory leads, the final crop of polls were roughly anticipating a tie.

Across the polls there appear to have been at least three errors:

1. Labour significantly underperformed compared with expectations set by polls. Support for

Miliband's party averaged 34% in the final polls, 3.5 points above the actual result. The figures for Ukip (12.5%), the Lib Dems (8%), and the Greens (4%) were within the polls' margins of error. Although the Conservatives' average in the final pre-election polls (34%) was also roughly three and a half points shy of the party's actual result, several companies – including Ipsos Mori, Opinium and ComRes – had the party's share on 35-36%.

2. The Lib Dems' result was catastrophic even in their strongholds. The party held on to only eight of their 57 seats, which is in stark contrast with the snapshots provided by constituency polling.

3. Although turnout saw a one-point increase on 2010, the level (66%) was significantly lower than that implied in most polls - this means the opinion of non-voters weighed on polling numbers.

The net effect of these trends was that Labour only gained 10 seats from the Tories, a quarter less than expected, and even lost eight constituencies to Cameron's party.

The collapse of the Lib Dems, which lost 26 seats to the Tories (more than double the expected number) and 12 to Labour (which, on the other hand, was in line with expectations), provided the Conservatives with the final push they needed to get over the line.

NOTES

CHAPTER TWO

HOW THE NEWS MEDIA COMPARE

London(CNN)"Pre-election polls in Britain's general election suggested the two main parties would be almost neck-and-neck after the May 7 vote, likely meaning a hung-parliament and days of political haggling to form a government.

They have instead been caught out by an outright majority for the Conservative Party.

Incumbent Prime Minister David Cameron's party took331 of Parliament's 650 seats compared to Labour's 232-- or 36.9% and 30.5%.

Is the nature of political polling such that American voters should take their own poll with a grain of salt in 2016?

Ahead of the 2012 U.S. elections, Nate Silver, from the website FiveThirtyEight, correctly predicted who would win all 50 states, even as pundits were saying the race was "too close to call." In 2008, he had also correctly projected all but one state.

As this year's British election results started trickling in, Silver tweeted that the world "may have a polling problem."

"Polls were bad in U.S. midterms, Scottish referendum, Israeli election and now tonight in UK," Silver said.

"UK polls herded toward all showing the same result as one another -- and that result turned out to be pretty wrong," he continued.

In a commentary on FiveThirtyEight, Silver suggested that forecasters had been overconfident. "Polls, in the UK and in other places around the world, appear to be getting worse as it becomes more challenging to contact a representative sample of voters. That means forecasters need to be accounting for a greater margin of error," he said.

SO WHAT WENT WRONG?

The final election poll released by the research company Ipsos MORI put the Conservatives ahead of Labour by 36 to 35%, indicating that "Britain may be on course for an indecisive general election result."

Ipsos MORI research director Gideon Skinner said researchers were still digesting the final election results.

"Obviously we'll need to carry out a review as we do after every election," he told CNN, "But we have to take a bit of a step back -- without wanting to gloss over it."

Skinner said many of Ipsos MORI predictions had come to pass, such as the poll for Scotland picking up the swing to the Scottish National Party.

"We have to appreciate what polls can do. National polls are not predictions of seats, they're snapshots of the parties' vote shares," he said.

"The Labour vote share is what we'll want to be concentrating on in our internal review. That clearly was an overestimation."

The Conservative win the UK election 2015 with a majority.

Polling company ComRes predicted that the Conservatives would win 35% of the vote, with Labour on 34%.

"We at ComRes have been saying all year that the Tories are ahead, Tom Mludzinski, ComRes' head of political polling, told CNN. "We've tried to be fairly bullish in saying that." "Clearly the Tories have outdone expectations and Labour underperformed."

Mludzinski said a number of factors could have played a role in the discrepancy, including undecided voters.

"We actually did a poll on the day of about 4,000 people, around 12-13% had made up their mind in the last 24 hours," he said. "The night before the election we had 20% saying they still might change their minds ... We'd like everyone to make up their minds nice and early."

Mludzinski said so-called "shy Tories "people not wanting to say they voted Conservative could also have been a factor as could the fragmentation of the vote between so many parties, but that there was no single reason for the difference in predictions and results.

"There clearly was an industry-wide issue in that no one really picked up the size of this win to the Conservatives," Mludzinski said.

In a blog post entitled "Poll Dancing," ComRes chairman Andrew Hawkins explained what he thought had happened, pointing out that pollsters had predicted percentages rather than seat numbers.

These had a plus or minus 3% margin of error and the poll on the election eve had been "statistically on the button," he said.

"We do indeed, together with academics and the media, need to look at how that vote share translates into House of Commons seats -- that is certainly true. But there is no need to throw the baby out with the bathwater. Most of the polls from most of the pollsters were within the margin of error. How they are interpreted and reported needs to be a matter of collective consideration," Hawkins said.

Pollsters Populus tweeted that the election results "raise serious issues" for pollsters.

"We will look at our methods and have urged the British Polling Council (an association of UK polling organizations) to set up a review."

The Polling Council later announced it was establishing an independent inquiry to examine "the possible causes of this apparent bias" and make recommendations for future polling.

Council president John Curtice -- Professor of Politics at Strathclyde University -- told CNN while polls should be judged on their percentages rather than seats and while it could well be true that many had fallen within their margins of error, an inquiry was still needed.

The polls had been accurate on the SNP, Liberal Democrats and Greens -- but they all had an error in the same direction, he said.

"The reason an inquiry has been set up is that actually the industry collectively clearly underestimated the Conservative lead over Labour," Curtice said.

"The thing above all you need to get right is the Conservative lead over Labour or vice versa because that is the most politically sensitive," he said. The miscalculation was one that had diminished but never entirely been eliminated, Curtice said. "(The inquiry) doesn't presume anything as to the explanation but it is clearly something the polling industry would profit from trying to understand."

Writing for The Conversation, Professors Paul Whiteley and Harold D. Clarke said election forecasters were "clearly losers" in the UK election.

"The usual health warnings were issued in the form of statistical uncertainty estimates, but these invitations to prudence were given less attention than they deserved by most consumers of the numbers," they said.

"Even with high quality survey data with huge sample sizes, predicting hundreds of constituency-level results in a first-past-the-post electoral system with varying patterns of inter-party competition remains a risky business. The 2015 election result forcefully illustrates the point."

Jacob Parakilas, the assistant project director for the U.S. Project at the London-based Chatham House think-tank told CNN that a lot of the difficulties and variants in the United Kingdom were down to the "increased complexities of UK elections relative to the U.S. elections."

"In presidential elections you have 50 constituencies and many of those are safe," he said, and whether a representative won by 15 or 20% was immaterial.

"At national level, during elections in the U.S. over the past 10-12 years the polls have been fairly accurate," he said. "The difference is that it's a lot easier to poll a two - party race."

There was a "fundamental difference" between the two systems, Parakilas said.

"Despite the fact that its much larger, the U.S. is an easier polling environment," he said. "The U.S. has gotten relatively polarized," he said. "I'm fairly confident that the numbers of people who cast split ballots have declined."

Prediction models for the U.S. elections had also become more reliable, Parakilas said, something he didn't believe had happened yet in the UK.

"While this will certainly be observed with interest by American pollsters and political observers, there are a lot of fundamental differences between the political systems in the two countries and the polling that has evolved," he said. "The direct impact might be limited in the U.S."

A pollster could get North Carolina totally wrong and still be right in Florida and it wouldn't matter. A national poll has much less use in the U.S. because it's meaningless.

STEPHEN COLLINSON OF CNN

CNN's Stephen Collinson also said polling had been more accurate in the U.S., pointing out that most public non-partisan polls ahead of the 2012 U.S. elections had gotten it right and that 2008 had been a similar story.

"The volume of polling in the U.S. is much deeper given that there are so many states, the election is so long and there are many more companies that poll. That gives a greater dataset to base predictions on -- it might make them less volatile."

But Collinson said pollsters in the U.S. sometimes had difficulty pinpointing exactly the profile for the electorate: "Before you can do a poll you have to work out what the electorate is and weight the poll accordingly."

Presidential challenger Mitt Romney hadn't read his electorate correctly in the 2012 race, Collinson said and his pollsters' predictions were thrown when more African Americans and Hispanics turned out to vote than expected. Romney campaign did not expect Obama's turn-out-the-vote results.

"I think there are always cautionary tales to be learned from polls and there are always abominations."

The abundance of polls in the United States meant there were also many averaging them out. "By doing that you can get a pretty good view of what the election is going to turn out like," Collinson said.

"In the UK, it's a disaster if they get a poll wrong because it's the whole country. In the U.S. it's state by state," he said.

"A pollster could get North Carolina totally wrong and still be right in Florida and it wouldn't matter. A national poll has much less use in the U.S. because it's meaningless."

The state-by-state division provided more of a "safety net" for pollsters, he said. "It's not just like one poll that's going to tell you everything."

Meanwhile, back in the UK, one polling company, Survation, said it was kicking itself for playing it too safe.

In a blog post "Snatching defeat from the jaws of victory," CEO Damian Lyons Lowe said its election eve poll had been close to the final result with the Conservatives on 37% and Labour on 31% (the final results were 36.9% to 30.4%).

"The results seemed so 'out of line' with all the polling conducted by ourselves and our peers -- what poll commentators would term an 'outlier' -- that I 'chickened out' of publishing the figures -- something I'm sure I'll always regret," he wrote.

But Lyons Lowe said there would be no internal review.

BBC NEWS

David Cameron has returned to Downing Street with the Tories having defied polls and won the general election.

The Conservatives made gains in England and Wales and are forecast by the BBC to secure 331 seats in the Commons, giving them a slender majority.

Labour leader Ed Miliband said he would stand down on Friday, saying his party must "rebuild" with a new leader.

Lib Dem leader Nick Clegg has also said he will quit, with his party set to be reduced from 57 to eight MPs.

UKIP leader Nigel Farage is also quitting after he failed to win Thanet South, losing by nearly 2,800 votes to the Conservatives.

In other election developments:

- The BBC forecast, with 643 of 650 seats declared, is Conservative 331, Labour 232, the Lib Dems 8, the SNP 56, Plaid Cymru 3, UKIP 1, the Greens 1 and others 19.

- The Conservatives are expected to get a 37% share of the national vote, Labour 31%, UKIP 13%, the Lib Dems 8%, the SNP 5%, the Green Party 4% and Plaid Cymru 1%.

- Mr Ed Miliband steps down after a "difficult and disappointing" night for Labour which saw Ed Balls lose and Jim Murphy and Douglas Alexander defeated by the SNP

- Nick Clegg said he would quit as leader after a "crushing" set of losses, which saw Vince Cable, Danny Alexander, David Laws, Simon Hughes and Charles Kennedy among a slew of Lib Dem casualties

- George Galloway, who was reported to the police for retweeting an exit pollbefore voting ended, has lost to Labour in Bradford West

- Nigel Farage has quit as UKIP leader after failing to be elected - although he may stand in the ensuing leadership contest. Douglas Carswell retained his Clacton seat

- Conservative minister Esther McVey was the highest-profile Tory loser, defeated by Labour in Wirral West

- The Green Party gets one seat after Caroline Lucas retains the Brighton Pavilion constituency she won in 2010

- Turnout is expected to be 66%, marginally up on 2010 and the highest since 1997

- Watch BBC election coverage and follow latest reaction

- Read more analysis from the BBC's experts

The Conservatives have now won over the 326 seats needed to form a majority administration, meaning they are able to govern without the need for a coalition or formal agreement with other parties.

Mr Cameron all but declared victory in a speech after being returned as MP for Witney, in which he set out his intention to press ahead with an in/out referendum on Britain's membership of the European Union and to complete the Conservatives' economic plan.

NOTES

CHAPTER THREE

HOW THE UNDER DOGS WON A MASSIVE VICTORY

The Tories Secret Weapons

1. THE MEDIA

There was a point in the election campaign – can you remember it? – When the Conservatives were struggling. Their solution was to come to the Guardian: offering at 5pm that Friday evening an authored piece by George Osborne.

The party was rattled after a week in which Labour had managed to get the media to talk about the same story, its plans to abolish non-dom status, for two whole days. The Tories had been stung, too, by the failure of their first attempt to move on, the preposterous attempt to argue that Ed Miliband was unfit to wield the nuclear button because five years earlier he had stood against his brother for the Labour leadership. Tack right, tack left – do the order of the directions matter? – seize the news: "Conservative party pledges extra £8bn a year for NHS".

The pace in a newsroom rarely flags, but in the high-speed six weeks of election campaigns a pattern quickly emerged. After a flurry of morning visits and lunchtime bulletins comes the gradual sound of *What next?* At 4pm, 5pm it is time to consider what the parties have to offer up to win the battle of tomorrow; not every joust is memorable. A Cameron offer to create 50,000 apprenticeships using a £227m fine imposed on Deutsche Bank made the Guardian front page on 28 April, seeing off a roughly repeated Labour promise to build 1m new homes by 2020 (page 8).

Barring a miracle, the news cycle lasts only 24 hours, starting with the overnight press beginning a battle to influence the BBC running order at 10pm, and that of Today. So, the Tories turned up every day fighting for the top story with promises about English laws (page 1), to freeze commuter fares (page 6) or to enshrine in law a promise to not to raise taxes in the next parliament (splash, Daily Telegraph). The last was a promise so gimmicky that the Guardian team thought it was not worthy of writing more than a sentence or two, until it turned out Labour had its own version of this idea involving an 8ft 6in stone. That was so silly thatsketch writer John Crace had to make the front page.

Labour undeniably had its good days: rent controls dominated the penultimate Sunday before the election.

A couple of well-judged interviews had been handed out the week before: US campaign guru David Axelrod led the Guardian, even though all he was doing was criticising the Tories for being "panic-stricken". That morning – 18 April – also saw Lord Falconer lift the lid on some of Labour's plans for government in the Times. There was the non-dom policy the Tories so hated five weeks out, but which Labour failed to return to until the last week, when the party belatedly began talking about it being one of its red lines days after Nick (who?) Clegg already crayoned in five of his own.

Controlled passion … the Tory campaign was a dispiriting exercise in media control.
Photograph: Toby Melville/AP

The point, though, is that they were not enough. Over the six weeks, the Tories just seemed to have more to throw at the late afternoon's blank canvas. And it wasn't the only area where the blues were ahead. Day after day, the Tories had contrived the photo opportunities so that there were Cameron than Miliband. The Guardian's picture desk had no choice but to put the prime minister and his hands in woad-like colouring on the front. Had the bacon sandwich and the second kitchen really done that much damage? Where were the Labour pictures from behind the scenes? It was even harder to find out what Team Labour was doing the next day, often it wasn't clear until well after 9pm; while the Tory "op note" had come through by 6pm.

Being beaten on energy and, arguably, organisation need not have mattered in the slightest either had Labour's campaign looked and sounded different. The Conservative campaign was a dispiriting masterclass in media control. Don't meet the public, lest they say something interesting; instead march from warehouse to factory to superstore lecturing supporters and workers mostly too scared to speak up (except for the woman apparently told off in Hendon by her line manager after asking the PM whether he had been at school with both Boris and Osborne). Only occasionally, by Jeremy Paxman or on Radio 1's Newsbeat, was the prime minister discomforted. Labour, too, adopted a similar approach, annoying the rightwing media by often excluding them (you need to woo everybody), when one might have tried something different … along the lines of Tony Blair's masochism strategy, or even the John Major soapbox.

The exception, of course, was Miliband's dalliance with Russell Brand, flawed because as a non-registered voter the comedian was an easy target. It was an intriguing encounter, although expectations ran ahead of themselves after the Miliband cavalcade was spotted outside Brand's flat and the video did not appear for a day and a half. But it turned out that one interview with a self-styled revolutionary was not going to win middle Britain around a week or so before the poll; in other words to defeat the Cameron machine a different tone needed to be more consistent.

David Cameron and his team including Craig Oliver (right) share a joke before receiving his constituency result in Witney. Photograph: Stefan Rousseau/PA

The Conservatives won the air game because they did better at controlling traditional media – look at how Craig Oliver mastered victory in the battle over the TV debates. Prime ministers may not be able to time the calling of elections, but they can decide in which TV formats they can take part. Oliver succeeded in ensuring the minor parties got ever more airtime in five-way, seven-way battles. And if it turned out that the Greens didn't do so well, it did not matter because Nicola Sturgeon did. Labour, it seemed, had to tag along.

Suddenly all the media wanted to talk about was coalition – because of the SNP's performance and the figures offered up by the pollsters. And lo there was a Tory scare story to plug that gap: that Labour would be dependent on the SNP to govern. A story that gained such traction that Miliband was forced to seize on the issue in the last of the TV non-debates; the Question Time where he said he did not want to be in government if it meant relying on the SNP. It was a position that supporters thought boxed him in a corner and still kept the issue at the top of the public's mind with a week to go.

There may be so much more to winning an election than the media battle over the last six weeks. But the striking successes of the Conservative air campaign cannot easily be ignored.

2. THE SOCIAL MEDIA POWERHOUSE

Share the facts: A game changer

HOW IT WORKED

Share the Facts was a great way that many conservative activists vigorously played **their** part in the campaign. By sharing videos, graphics and blog posts with friends, **they** helped get the message out about everything that the Tories were doing to secure a brighter future – and how Labour would put it all at risk.

Every week, Share the Facts users helped the Conservative Party reach over 3 million people. That's massive campaigning power tool.

Activists get points for every post they share – with rewards for those doing most to support the campaign.

EARNING POINTS

You were awarded points for 3 things:

Sharing a post – you immediately receive the number of points shown on the post

When your friends click the post you've shared – 10 extra points

When your friends react to your post (i.e. like, share or retweet) – 10 extra points

You could just Click "MY SHARES" to see how many points each share has earned, and click "LEADERBOARD" to see your overall score and position on the leaderboard.

To get started, you click on the "SHARE NOW" button at the end of any Share the Facts post. If you're not logged in, you'll immediately be prompted to do so.

If you have a Facebook account, you can just click "Log in with Facebook" to get started. If you don't use Facebook, click "Sign Up Now" and you'll be asked for some basic details to set up a Conservatives.com account instead.

Now you're ready to share your first post. Click on the "SHARE NOW" button at the end of the specific post you want to share. Before sharing, you'll need to connect a social media account (Facebook, Twitter or LinkedIn).

You only have to do this once and you can connect as many accounts as you like. The more accounts you connect, the more points you'll be able to earn.

Once that's done, type whatever message you'd like to appear alongside your shared post and click "SHARE". Alternatively, you can click "SCHEDULE" to share the post at a time of your choosing.

Please note that you can only share an individual post ONCE per social network

THE MOBILE APP

If you want the best possible Share the Facts experience, please download and install the Share the Facts app for your iPhone or Android device. The app sends the latest posts straight to your phone, and enables sharing to all your social networks with just one click.

HOW I BECAME THE TOP LEADER AND 7 TIMES WINNER OF TOP PRIZES ON SHARE THE FACTS
BY JOSHUA JOGO

Above some prestigious prizes won by the author from Share The Facts!

I signed up to share the facts on 24th June 2014 and began to share posts from the platform to my social media contacts. I won my first prize in January 2015 finishing top 20 for the first time. (I finished 4th on this occasion). This invigorated my spirit and soul to do something more. So I decided that I will be top winner of the prize the following month and mobilised all my social media contacts to "share the facts". This won me the top prize and thereafter became the man to beat. I went on to win the top prize each week in the run up to the election.

I won seven amazing prizes and accumulated a record 1.5 million (1,512,711) in share points.

I had really wanted to go on the Road Trips and Join the Battle Bus. However, because I was running as a council candidate myself that meant that I needed to campaign locally in my constituency of Spelthorne to win our much needed victory there.

Additionally, I was actively involved with Team2015 and attended several campaign events in very marginal seats that were later won by the conservatives.

ANY OTHER QUESTIONS

If you have any other questions about Share the Facts, or have a suggestion about how to improve the site, please send us an email using the Conservatives.com Contact Us form.

3. THE BATTLE BUS

Battlebus2015 fuelled and ready for victory!
The battles kicked off on 14th April 2015 at 7:2 am and was fuelled and ready for victory!

This was from the team that brought to us the Roadtrip2015 action days over the past year now launching a brand new initiative for the final stretch of the election campaign. Battlebus2015 will be taking teams all across the country to the most marginal Conservative seats to talk to voters and show them that the best action for Britain is to vote Conservative on 7th of May 2015.

Battlebus2015 founder, Mark Clarke, had this to say. "It has been too long since we used the concept of Battlebuses for our activists during elections. Maggie had one, and she won three elections, so it seems sensible to bring back this icon of Conservatism.

Parliament Street's very own Chairman- Patrick Sullivan- has joined Roadtrip2015 on a number of bus based action weekends which were not only brilliant fun, but also highly effective and beneficial for the constituencies visited. Patrick will be joined the Battlebus2015 team, and top Conservative figures, on the road and this became one of the major victory boast for the conservatives.

The buses will be ran from 26th April – 6th May and were be based in Tamworth and Glastonbury/Taunton. They campaigned all week visiting up to three seats a day. By campaigning mid-week, people can join their local teams at the weekend. Based from the centre of the country, almost every seat will was reachable" Mark explains. With the focus of the Battlebus being to reach swing voters in our most marginal areas, the initiative looks set to make a real difference to the results of the election.

Roadtrip2015: a typical battle bus road trip schedule and advert.

Sunday, April 26, 2015 at 4:00 PM - Wednesday, May 6, 2015 at 7:00 PM (BST)

Ticket Information

TICKET TYPE	SALES END	PRIZE	FEE	QUANTITY
26th April-1st May	Ended	£50.00	£3.65	N/A
1st May-6th May	Ended	£50.00	£3.65	N/A
26th April-6th May	Ended	£100.00	£6.65	N/A

Enter promotional code

Who's Going

Connect to see which of your Facebook friends are going.

Connect with Facebook

Share Battlebus2015

Share Tweet

Event Details

Following the fantastic success of our campaign days in the past year, Roadtrip2015 is delighted to invite you to join us in the final weeks of the General Election campaign, for this once in a lifetime opportunity, as we take Battlebus2015 all over the country for our brilliant candidates, hoping to hold current seats and win new ones!

We will be running two buses for ten action packed days where we will based in Tamworth and Taunton/Glastonbury, travelling from here to seats all over the country. You can join us for the full ten days, or the first or last 5 days.

Once you have selected the dates you wish join us for from the ticket options, you will be able to select the location you wish to be based at in the next step of the registration process.

We cannot do this without your help, so whether you can join us for one of the five day periods or both, be sure to sign up today to secure your place!

We ask for a payment of just £50 (£25 for students) which will be small contribution towards the hotel costs. We will meet ALL the remaining hotel costs and ALL the food costs and provide FREE transport to the Battlebus2015 hotel from London.

This exclusive opportunity will allow you to experience the buzz of the election on a national scale, and take part in the campaigns of many constituencies. We expect many leading figures in our Party to join the bus for different days.
If you are a student please click 'Enter promotional code' and use 'student' to claim 50% off the ticket prize!

If you would like to book your own room, please contact india.brummitt@conservatives.com to discuss availability after you have booked your ticket
Have questions about Battlebus2015? Contact Roadtrip2015

David Cameron hops off his battle bus to greet Michelle Donelan, Conservative prospective MP for Chippenham

Day one set the tone for David Cameron's campaign for another term as prime minister. Every moment was carefully planned and controlled, from the formalities at Westminster to the first rally at a target seat in Wiltshire.

When I covered his election campaign five years ago, David Cameron was the opposition leader offering hope and a fresh start after 13 years of Labour government. Now he is fighting on his record of five tough years in power. He is trying to make a virtue of that fact, though some in his party want a more optimistic, upbeat message.

His favourite phrase of a "long-term economic plan" has already been rehearsed at numerous sessions of prime minister's questions, media appearances and "Cameron direct" meetings with the public.

It is central to the core message which Mr Cameron delivered on Monday and will be repeated across the country over the next six weeks.
Out of media player. Press enter to return or tab to continue.
Media caption The BBC's Carole Walker takes a look inside the Conservative Party campaign bus, as they head to their first campaign rally

He will say that the Conservatives' economic policies are cutting the deficit, reducing unemployment and creating economic growth.

He will warn that Labour would put that at risk and bring economic chaos. And he will set out the "stark choice" of either himself or Ed Miliband holding the reins of power in Downing Street.

The first rally of the campaign was at a school at Chippenham in Wiltshire, where the Conservatives are hoping to overturn Duncan Hames's Liberal Democrat majority of just over 2,400.

David Cameron speaks at a rally at a school in Wiltshire

Mr Cameron - jacket off, sleeves rolled up - spoke for no more than 10 minutes to about 300 Tory activists in a small school hall, then headed straight back to London. That was sufficient to deliver the key lines in time for the evening television bulletins and Tuesday's papers.

The tussle of the day was over the Tory leader's claim that Labour would cost working families £3,000 in higher taxes. Labour dismissed it, the respected Institute for Fiscal Studies questioned the basis for the assertion, but the Tories said they stood by their figure. Such arguments are the daily fodder of elections - rarely do they have much overall impact on voters.

The next big test will be Thursday's televised debate. Tory strategists know it's a risky event, with Mr

Cameron lined up alongside six opponents. They will be hoping it does not upset their carefully-laid plans for the next six weeks.

WINNERS AND LOOSERS:

A night of ecstatic joy with despair and agonizing anguish.

Election2015: How David Cameron's Conservatives won. Tory success attributed to one of most disciplined, focused and ruthless campaigns in history of British politics. Here's how they did it...

Prime Minister David Cameron and his wife Samantha are applauded by staff upon entering 10 Downing Street Photo: PA

David Cameron has won the election and returned to Downing Street with an outright majority after Labour was virtually wiped out by the SNP in Scotland and the Liberal Democrat vote collapsed.

Ed Miliband, Nick Clegg and Nigel Farage all stood down in the space of an hour as the Conservatives reached 323 seats while Labour's vote slumped.

The Conservative victory was the product of one of the most tightly-controlled electoral campaigns in British history. Here's how they did it: Ed Miliband will 'dance to SNP tune'

In the wake of the independence referendum, Lynton Crosby - the Conservatives' campaign chief - was quick to spot that the risk that Labour would try to squeeze into power with the support of the SNP.

This rapidly became one of the Tories' main lines of attack and, during the election campaign, effectively drowned out Labour's key messages.

Backed by polls suggesting a landslide for the SNP in Scotland, David Cameron and his team repeatedly hammered home their message about the threat Ed Miliband poised to the Union.

In the final weeks of the campaign, the message was reinforced by Sir John Major, the former Prime Minister, who said Ed Miliband must rule out a deal with the SNP.

Labour floundered as it tried to respond. For weeks, Ed Miliband tried to duck the question of whether he was prepared to do a deal, claiming that he was instead focused on securing a majority.

It was only in the final week of the campaign that Mr Miliband finally ruled out a deal, by which time the damage had already been done.

After months of preparation, Labour's pitch to voters was based on two central messages: the threat the Tories posed to the NHS and the cost of living crisis.

In the critical short campaign, however, Labour's attempts to put its two crucial messages front and centre were disrupted by the SNP question.

'LONG-TERM ECONOMIC PLAN'

The Tories' strength on the economy was at the heart of the party's election victory.

The foundations for their success were laid in 2010 when the party exploited Labour's implosion after Gordon Brown's defeat to attack Labour's economic record.

"They are the party that crashed the economy," the message ran. "We are the ones with the long-term economic plan."

Over the course of the Coalition, the Tories built their economic credibility under George Osborne by cutting spending and implementing austerity measures.

As a result, Britian has enjoyed the fastest rate of growth in the G7 group of developed countries with record numbers of jobs.

POLICY EXPLAINER: DEFICIT PARTY STANCE...

- Conservative: Eliminate the deficit and leave a minor budget surplus by 2019/2020.

- Labour: Balance the books and have national debt falling as soon as possible within the next Parliament.

- Liberal Democrats: Raising an extra £6bn in tax rises and £6bn from tax dodgers. Structural deficit gone by 2017.

- Ukip: Raise 40p threshold to £55,000, personal allowance to £13,000 and cut foreign aid by £9 billion.

- Green: Clamp down on tax avoidance and introduce "much-needed" extra green taxes.

- SNP: "Modest" increase in public spending, protecting NHS budget and creating more jobs.

Government spending could fall to its lowest since 1999

Strong ground for the Conservatives who rightly identify Labour's record on the deficit as a weak spot. But both big parties need to give much more detail about their fiscal plans after the election. Voters deserve to know just what they are voting for here.

The messaging from the Tories was relentless. Jim Messina, the former White House strategist who advised the Tories, told MPs that every day they failed to campaign on the economy was a day wasted.

Labour attempted to reassert its own economic credibility by belatedly committing to austerity measures itself.

It fought the election on the basis of the cost-of-living crisis, claiming that the economic recovery wasn't working for ordinary people.

In the end, the Tories' economic message was stronger.

The Cameron factor

The Tories have always been acutely aware that David Cameron is significantly more popular than his own party.

Labour, on the other hand, have been afflicted by the opposite problem - Ed Miliband is significantly less popular than his party.

The Conservatives spent the run-up to the election repeatedly questioning Mr Miliband's fitness to lead Britain.

The attacks were sharpened after a series of gaffes by the Labour leader, which culminated in a picture of him eating a bacon sandwich.

However, at the start of the campaign, Mr Miliband appeared to recover his poise and begin to win credibility.

During the leaders debate he revelled in his "geek" status and even became a pin up for some teenage girls.

His personal ratings, however, told a different story. While people's trust in Mr Miliband improved, his overall net ratings were negative and far behind those Mr Cameron.

Mr Cameron, in the meantime, raised his game. Having been accused of lacking emotion, he delivered a series of passionate speeches in the final week of the campaign.

"I'm pumped up," he repeatedly said with his sleeves rolled up. The approach appears to have worked.

LIBERAL DEMOCRAT DECAPITATION STRATEGY

The Tories were remorseless in the way they attacked their former Coalition partners.

Having worked closely alongside them for five years, they went for the jugular during the election campaign.

Of the 23 seats they targeted to win the election, 22 were held by Liberal Democrats, many by former government colleagues.

In the short campaign Mr Cameron repeatedly visited Liberal Democrat target seats in the South West.

Nick Clegg, the Liberal Democrat leader, dismissed the Tory strategy as "fantasy" and and a "fib".

He, and many pollsters and commentators, believed that the "incumbancy factor" of sitting MPs would be enough to see them through.

He could not have been more wrong. For Mr Cameron, it was a moment to savour and the "sweetest victory of all".

"There are so many things to savour," he told Conservative activists, including "the fact that every election we always think we are going to displace those Lib Dems in the West Country and we have finally done that."

However George Osborne, the Chancellor, had a little more compassion for Danny Alexander, the former Lib Dem chief secretary to the Treasury. "I worked very closely with him and was sad to see him go," he said.

Relentless discipline

The Tory election machine was both feared and admired by its rivals. During the 2010 election campaign, the party chopped and changed its approach.

This time, there was a steely focus under the ever watchful eye of Mr Crosby. "There were no screw ups, we had a plan and we stuck to it," said one source. "A lot of that is down to Lynton".

While the rigidity of the campaign might have frustrated commentators, it worked. Eurosceptic back-benchers, in the meantime, were left relatively placated by the prospect of an EU referendum.

So while Labour was riven by in-fighting, the Tories were focused.

David and Samantha Cameron leaving Downing Street after rousing election victory

Senior party sources say that the most dangerous moment of the campaign came when Jean Claude-Juncker, the President of the EU Commission, said that there could be no limits on freedom of movement.

"Even the most ardent Eurosceptics didn't get involved," one source said.

Whether back-benchers will remain so restrained now they find themselves with more power remains to be seen.

General Election 2015: the key moments

Telegraph front page

Cameron will hold on to power, say exit polls

Party leaders to set differences aside for VE Day commemoration

xit poll puts the Conservatives ahead on 316 seats, with Labour on 239 seats, the Liberal Democrats on 10, the SNP on 58 and Ukip on two.

First result declared: 23.16am

Labour win the first seat to declare in the 2015 General Election with an increased majority for Bridget Phillipson in Houghton and Sunderland South.

First key seat: 1.52am

Conservatives comfortably hold Nuneaton - one of Labour's key target seats - with 20,827 votes to Labour's 15,945.

Youngest MP since 1667

Labour shadow foreign secretary Douglas Alexander loses his Paisley and Renfrewshire South seat in the House of Commons to 20-year-old SNP candidate Mhairi Black and the **Scottish bloodbath begins.**

Labour loses Gordon Brown's former seat in Scotland, the Kirkcaldy and Cowdenbeath constituency, to the SNP.

Murphy's seat falls too: Scottish Labour leader Jim Murphy loses his East Renfrewshire seat to the SNP's Kirsten Oswald.

Lib Dem collapse begins: Simon Hughes, a senior Liberal Democrat and MP of 32 years' standing, loses in Bermondsey and Old Southwark to Labour by around 5,000 votes.

Ukip's sole win: Ukip wins its first seat in a General Election, with former Conservative MP Douglas Carswell seeing a much reduced majority compared to last year's by-election.

Liberal Democrat Business Secretary Vince Cable loses his Twickenham seat to the Conservatives.

Nick Clegg just holds on: Lib Dem leader Nick Clegg holds onto his Sheffield Hallam seat. He said he would be discussing his leadership with colleagues after a "cruel and punishing night for his party".

Labour leader Ed Miliband, who retains his Doncaster North seat, says: "This has clearly been a very difficult and disappointing night for the Labour Party.

DANNY ALEXANDER LOSSES

Accepting victory in his Witney constituency, David Cameron says: "This is clearly a very strong night for the Conservative Party. We've had a positive response to a positive campaign."

Former Liberal Democrat Chief Secretary to the Treasury Danny Alexander loses the Inverness, Nairn, Badenoch and Strathspey seat to the SNP's Drew Hendry.

Ed Balls loses his seat

Ed Balls becomes the biggest casualty of the night, losing his Morley and Outwood constituency in Leeds to the Conservatives by 422 votes after a recount. "Any personal disappointment I have at this result is as nothing as compared to the sense of sorrow I have at the result Labour has achieved across the UK tonight, he said.

NIGEL FARAGE FAILS TO WIN SOUTH THANET

Nigel Farage, the Ukip leader, fails to win Thanet South from the Conservatives. He resigns soon afterwards, insisting he has "never felt happier", with a "weight lifted off his shoulders" - but that he may return to contest leadership in September.

Emotional Nick Clegg calls defeat 'crushing'

Nick Clegg resigns as leader of the Liberal Democrats. In a tearful speech, he says the Lib Dems had suffered a "catastrophic" defeat. "Clearly the results have been immeasurably more crushing and unkind than I could ever have feared. For that I must take responsibility," he told his party.

Ed Miliband resigns as Labour leader saying he takes "absolute and total responsibility" for the party's defeat. "I'm so sorry for all those colleagues who lost their seats," he said, in a dignified speech that included jokes about his own image and "the most unlikely cult of the 21st Century, Milifandom". Early favourites to succeed him include Andy Burnham, Yvette Cooper and Chuka Umunna.

David Cameron announces he will form a new government after visiting the Queen at Buckingham Palace following his resounding victory that delivered the Conservatives an outright majority for the first time since 1992. He promised voters "we are on the brink of something special in this country" – and that he will deliver his election pledge to hold an EU referendum.

WHY THE 'EDSTONE' BECAME LABOUR'S TOMBSTONE

Labour's 'vague' promises are 'not worth what they are written on', says director of company which carved the plinth.

Labour will "rue the day" it ordered the party's manifesto pledges to be carved in rock, the man who made the eight-foot stone plinth has said.

Ed Miliband faced criticism after in the final week of the general election campaign after unveiling a huge limestone block with the party's key manifesto pledges carved into it.

Steve Vanhinsbergh, director of Stone Circle, which carved the plinth - dubbed the "EdStone" - said it was full of "vague" promises and that are "not worth what they are written on".

Labour aides at the time said that they would erect the stone in the Downing Street garden when they won the election.

In the wake of David Cameron's majority election victory, senior Tory strategists said that they reacted with glee when the former leader unveiled the plinth, describing it as a "tombstone".

• Labour's 'Ed Stone' found hidden at an industrial estate called Westminster
• #EdStone: the social media reaction to Ed Miliband's manifesto monument
• Where is #EdStone? The monumental question facing Labour after Miliband's departure

Mr Vanhinsbergh told the BBC: "History is written by the winners and the Labour Party will rue the day they ordered the EdStone to be made. "If you read what is written there closely they are all so vague. They are not worth what they are written on."

Asked why he voted Tory, he added: "Conservatives generally are more pro-business and I was a little bit worries about Labour's policies with regard to business."

Mr Miliband unveiled the EdStone in a car park in Hastings the weekend before the vote.

He said it was to prove to voters that he would follow through on all his manifesto pledges.

Meanwhile, Bob Roberts, one of Mr Miliband's closest aides, blamed a "tidal wave" of nationalism in Scotland for Labour's general election defeat.

Mr Roberts, one of Mr Miliband's communications directors, conceded that the party should have done "more on economic reassurance".

However, he appeared to place most of the blame on people in Scotland, who wiped out Labour north of the border in the election by voting in huge numbers for the SNP.

He said: "The big change in Scotland, the big rise in nationalism was what really hurt us.

"We perhaps needed to do more on economic reassurance but I think, in the end, it was a huge structural shift - a tidal wave in Scotland - which we got caught up in."

The final weeks were dominated by a debate over whether Mr Miliband would attempt to form a minority government which would have relied on votes from SNP MPs.

Mr Roberts also admitted that Labour left it "too late" to "challenge" the narrative that it was Labour that "crashed" the UK economy the last time it was in power.

Mr Miliband repeatedly during the campaign refused to apologise for Labour's borrowing during Gordon Brown's government.

At the final televised debate, he was accused of "lying" by members of the audience for failing to admit the last Labour government's economic failings.

NOTES

CHAPTER FIVE

BIG VICTOR IN SURREY

Election results: Conservative clean sweep in Surrey as David Cameron leads party to majority

Tory general election win described as "an unprecedented vote of confidence in David Cameron's leadership"

Conservative candidates proved unstoppable at the general election in Surrey again, retaining all seats as their party headed for a surprise majority in Parliament.

In what had been forecast as the most "unpredictable election in years", with Labour and the Tories supposedly neck-and-neck, the outlook suddenly changed when an exit poll late on Thursday put the Conservatives very close to winning an overall majority.

The result led to Ed Miliband resigning as Labour leader, with the SNP wiping out his party in Scotland, while Nick Clegg also bowed out of the top job with the Liberal Democrats after a crushing night.

Conservative MPs were all re-elected in Surrey's 11 constituencies - Guildford, Woking, Mole, Surrey Heath, South West Surrey, Runnymede & Weybridge, Walton, Spelthorne, East Surrey, Reigate and Epsom & Ewell.

But there were gains for UKIP in East Surrey, where the party more than doubled its number of votes, with Helena Windsor coming in second behind Sam Gyimah.

Chris Grayling was "delighted" after he retained his Epsom & Ewell seat with 33,309 votes.

"It is a huge honour to be elected as Member of Parliament and to serve this area," he said.

"It's been a matter of great pride to do so for the last 14 years and has been a great pleasure."

Surrey's 11 Conservative MPs

Anne Milton kept her Guildford seat with 30,802 votes, saying: "I'm overwhelmed, honoured and privileged to get that sort of vote of confidence.

"Every vote counts and every vote is an act of faith in your ability to represent people."

The HG Wells centre in Woking erupted with cheers after it was announced that Jonathan Lord had retained his seat for the Tories with 56% of the vote.

Speaking to *Get Surrey* after his win, Mr Lord said: "I'm pretty tired and exhausted but absolutely delighted and thrilled with the results and a little humbled as well.

"This does exceed my wildest expectations and for 29,000 people in Woking and the surrounding areas to put their faith in me in Parliament for another five years is a fantastic feeling."

Sir Paul Beresford won his fifth consecutive election in Mole Valley, holding the seat with a majority of more than 25,000 votes.

He said: "We will continue to work, like we have been, to get this country back on its feet.

"We need to get the deficit down, we need to get borrowing down.

"I do not want to hand over an enormous debt to my children."

There was much pre-election talk about a potential National Health Party challenge to Health Secretary Jeremy Hunt in South West Surrey, but he triumphed with 34,199 votes.

"I am absolutely thrilled," he said. "No MP can ever take his majority for granted and the idea of a safe seat is gone.

"I hope I will always be a local campaigning MP, who is as much involved in the local issues as the national one."

Kwasi Kwarteng hailed an "extraordinary" triumph for the Conservatives as he secured a second term as MP for Spelthorne, while Crispin Blunt - re-elected in Reigate - said voters had given Prime Minister David Cameron a "handsome mandate to allow [him] to continue with the work he has been doing".

Dominic Raab put his victory in Esher & Walton down to "hard work, elbow grease and a great team around me".

And in Runnymede & Weybridge, Philip Hammond was "delighted" to be elected for a fifth term.

Michael Gove cruised to victory in Surrey Heath again with 32,582 votes and told the BBC that the exit poll indications - which were confirmed by Friday lunchtime - were "an unprecedented vote of confidence in David

Cameron's leadership, and in particular the message that if you want to secure the economic recovery then you have got to make sure that he is in Downing Street".

Conservative Kwasi Kwarteng held his Spelthorne seat with more than 24,000 votes.

Mr Kwarteng beat his nearest rival UKIP's Redvers Cunningham into second place with 10,234 votes.

He first won the seat in 2010 when he replaced David Wilshire with a majority of 10,019.

Scoring 24,386 votes he has now increased his majority to 14,152.

Labour's Rebecca Geach came in third with 9,114 votes with the Liberal Democrat's Rosie Shimell in fourth with 3,163.

The Green Party's Paul Jacobs was fifth with 1,724, with Independent Juliet Griffith in sixth with 230 votes.

Trade Union and Socialist Coalition candidate Paul Couchman came in seventh place with 228 votes.

Speaking after the result, Mr Kwarteng thanked his campaign team for their rough and ready effective methods.

"This election 2015 across the whole country has been extraordinary," he said.

"I can't remember an election where a government in power for five years to then win more seats.

"I hope we can get some good results in tomorrow's borough election."

CHAPTER SIX

THE OFFICIAL OPENING OF PARLIAMENT
THE QUEEN'S SPEECH

By David Cameron

"When we came to office in 2010, Britain was on the brink. Our task was urgent: to rescue our economy from the mire. With that economy now going in the right direction, we are once again on the brink - but this time, on the brink of something special.

We have a golden opportunity to renew the idea that working people are backed in this country; to renew the promise to those least fortunate that they will have the opportunity for a brighter future; and to renew the ties that bind every part of our United Kingdom. We now have the mandate to deliver that renewal.

And it starts with today's Queen's Speech: a clear programme for working people, social justice, and bringing our country together - put simply, a One Nation Queen's Speech from a One Nation Government.

The first task of a One Nation Government is to help all working people have security. And nothing is more crucial to that than a job. A new Bill will help to create two million more jobs this Parliament. That means there should be a job for everyone who wants one - in other words, full employment. To help people get those jobs, we'll train them up; three million more will start apprenticeships over the next five years.

We will also reward work by letting people keep even more of the money they earn - for the first time putting it into law that the Minimum Wage is and always will be tax free. That will be alongside a five-year tax lock which means there will be no income tax, VAT or National Insurance rate rises in this Parliament.

The second big focus of this Queen's Speech is championing social justice. That starts with education: a decent schooling for every child, no matter where they're from. Our school reforms in the last Parliament were bold; one million more children are now learning in good or outstanding schools.

In this Parliament they will be bolder still: taking over and turning into Academies not just failing schools but coasting ones too, as part of our new Education and Adoption Bill; opening not just a few more Free Schools, but 500 more. Of course, there is nothing that embodies the spirit of One Nation and the cause of social justice more than our NHS, which is there for everyone, whoever they are, regardless of their ability to pay. So we will continue increasing spending on our health service, by at least £8 billion a year by 2020, and make it a truly 7-day NHS.

We will also continue our welfare reforms that help people into jobs, reducing the benefit cap further, to £23,000. Our reforms will incentivise work - so people are always better off after a day at the office or factory than they would have been sitting at home.

That's true social justice - not handing people benefit cheque after benefit cheque with no end in sight, but turning workless households into working households; the misery of unemployment into the purpose and dignity of employment; and the welfare system into a lifeline, not a way of life.

Third, this Queen's Speech will bring every part of our United Kingdom together. Our legislation will make sure this recovery reaches everyone, from the oldest industrial towns to the remotest rural villages. Our High Speed 2 Bill will help bring our great northern cities together in a Northern Powerhouse that rivals the biggest cities in the world.

For our different nations and regions to coexist as One Nation, people must have more direct power over the areas in which they live. So our Cities Devolution Bill will allow them to bid for an elected mayor, with far more sway over planning, transport, policing and health. We will have a Scotland Bill, a Wales Bill and a Northern Ireland Bill, and will put into practice our promises on devolution - making Holyrood the most powerful devolved Parliament in the world. Governing with respect means respecting the wishes of the English too.

That's why we will address the fundamental unfairness devolution causes in England, by introducing English votes for English laws. And the UK will have more control over its affairs, as we bring forward proposals for a British Bill of Rights to replace the Human Rights Act.

We will also legislate to have an EU Referendum before the end of 2017, putting the question to the British people for the first time in 40 years: the European Union - in or out. Underpinning all of this is security. With an Extremism Bill, an Investigatory Powers Bill and a Policing and Criminal Justice Bill, we will keep our people safe.

That's our legislative programme. It's challenging but doable; optimistic but realistic. It's the bold first step of a One Nation Government - a Government for working people.

And this is the Britain we're setting out to create: a Britain where you can get a decent job, have a good education, buy a home of your own, have dignity when you retire, and feel safe and secure throughout your life. In the last Parliament we laid the foundations for that; in this Parliament we will use them to build something special. We've now got the majority we need. With this Queen's Speech we're going to get on and do it - for every single person in this great nation.

So -if you haven't already - please join the Conservative Party today, and play your part in everything we'll achieve together in the next five years.

Thank you."

David Cameron